The Dalesman Book of
Country Recipes

The Dalesman Book of
Country Recipes

Dalesman Books 1983

The Dalesman Publishing Company Ltd.,
Clapham, via Lancaster, LA2 8EB

First published 1983

© Dalesman Publishing Company Ltd., 1983

ISBN: 0 85206 757 7

Phototypeset, printed and bound by Galava Printing Company Ltd., Nelson, Lancs.

Contents

Cover design by Barbara Yates. Drawings in the text by Valary Gustard, E. Jeffrey, David Nash, J.J. Thomlinson and Barbara Yates. Photographs courtesy Flour Advisory Bureau and The Cranberry Centre.

Introduction

COUNTRY COOKING has traditionally been characterised as plain, simple and wholesome. Many people have drawn up chairs to enjoy high tea when there did not appear to be too much on the table, only to discover that the cakes and scones and pies were made with such substantial ingredients that there was still plenty left when their appetites had been satisfied. Main dishes have always been substantial, well suited to the needs of a largely agricultural population living where the air is often as tingling fresh as wine brought straight up from the cellar.

In former times every country household would have its own recipe book, handwritten and often with a bias towards cakes. Such collections provide the basis for the first and last sections in this book: 'Recipes from a Country Kitchen'—originally tried and tested in a 17th century Dales farmhouse, and 'Christmas Recipes'—handed down to Anne R. Burkett over several generations.

The sandwich between these two sections is provided by favourite country recipes which have been sent in by Dalesman readers down the years. These include the very best of farmhouse cooking in the form of some mouth-watering meat and savoury dishes.

We thank all contributors and readers who have helped in the preparation of this book. Through their generosity many fine recipes are now shared with people living far and wide.

Users of this book are particularly recommended to consult the table of oven settings overleaf and the index on pages 78 - 80.

Oven Settings

Some of the recipes in this book use traditional descriptions for oven settings. The conversion factors for electric and gas ovens are as follows:-

	Electric	Gas
Very Slow	250	1
Slow	300	2
Moderate	350	4
Hot (or Quick)	400	6
Very Hot	475	8

1. *Recipes from a Country Kitchen*

by Kathleen Inglis

Recipes from a Country Kitchen

by Kathleen Inglis

MANY of the following recipes are taken from the 'Scrapbook' kept by my grandfather William Bowdin, whose family came from Hole Bottom Farm, Hebden, in the Yorkshire Dales. They were famous musicians and formed a local orchestra. Later entries in the 'Scrapbook' are by my grandmother, while I have also included some recipes that are my own, were handed down to me by my mother Laura Louise Bowdin or have been passed on to me by my friends.

COLD BRISKET OF BEEF

4 lbs of plain brisket
Salt
Water

A lean piece of brisket should be boned and tied into a good shape by the butcher. Sprinkle a little salt between the rolls of meat. The cooking is done in a saucepan in the oven, very slowly, for five hours. Make sure that the lid fits tightly and, though the meat can nearly touch the sides of the pan, there must be ample space above to avoid any chance of that lid being pushed off. Add ½ pint of cold water and cook at 300°. From time to time check that the meat is very gently simmering. Should it reach boiling point reduce the temperature to 250°. Remove from the oven at the end of the five hours, take off the lid but leave the meat to cool in the pan. When thoroughly cold put in the fridge overnight and, in the morning, the fat can be easily removed with a spoon, to reveal the brisket sitting in its own ready-made glaze.

(This recipe saw me and my family through the war—it was by far the best buy our ration books could produce and even the dripping made pastry or gingerbread).

BEEF ROLL

1½ lbs minced steak
¼ lb minced ham
1 egg
¼ lb breadcrumbs
Pepper
Salt
A very little cayenne

Mix the minced steak and ham with the bread-crumbs, with a fork. Beat the seasoning into the egg (then one person won't get all the cayenne). Add this to the meat and mix thoroughly. This roll used to be steamed in a straight-sided stoneware marmalade pot but, since these have become collector's pieces nowadays, you will probably have to do as I do, just settle for a well-greased bowl. Cover with greased grease-proof paper, then foil, and steam for 1½ hours. Turn out carefully and roll in browned bread-crumbs.

SALMON SHAPE

1lb tin salmon
2 eggs (beaten well)
4 tablespoons melted butter
1 tea-cup breadcrumbs
Salt
Pepper
Cayenne (watch it!)
Mustard (still go carefully)
Milk

With a fish fork remove the bones and skin from the salmon, break it up and add the bread-crumbs, then the eggs into which you have mixed the seasoning and beaten well, then the melted butter and finally mix in enough milk to reach what cooks call a soft dropping consistency (a spoonful will readily slip back into the bowl). Transfer to a well-greased bowl, cover with greased greaseproof paper, then foil, and steam for 1½ hours.

This is a useful recipe. It is good served hot with a suitable sauce, mashed or new potatoes and peas, if liked. It is equally good cold, preferably with cucumber and a green salad.

SALMON—to cook

Put into boiling water. Boil five minutes. Add two breakfast cups cold water, and simmer. Leave in water for five minutes after cooking, as this improves the flavour.

Slice weighing 1lb takes ¼ hour
Slice weighing 3lbs takes 25 minutes
Slice weighing 6lbs takes 40 minutes
Grilse 7 to 8lbs takes half an hour

MEAT JELLY PIE

2lb shin of beef
1 bay leaf
½ onion
Pepper and salt (Be sparing—remember that a stock cube contains seasoning)
Gelatine
Stock

SHORTCRUST PASTRY
8oz plain flour (sieved)
Salt
4oz soft margarine
2 tablespoons cold water

This is a well flavoured cold pie, the meat being cooked by itself first, allowed to set in a jelly from which all fat can be removed then baked the next day when the pastry has been added. So, choose a pie dish which can be covered during the first stage, or transfer the meat, while still hot, from an ovenware casserole if need be, to a pie dish.

Cut the shin into medium-sized pieces, removing as much fat as possible, add chopped onion, a little pepper and salt and the bay leaf and cover with good stock. (A stock cube will be

13

suitable). Cook in the oven slowly, say 300° for three hours at least. Take a look now and then to be sure that boiling point has not been reached. It must just simmer. If need be reduce heat to 250°. Remove from oven, remember to add the pie funnel, and take out a small bowl of gravy in which to add a packet of gelatine, to ensure a good jelly set, returning this to the pie dish when dissolved. When quite cold, put in the fridge for the night, removing any fat in the morning.

Pastry: The original recipe is for a hot water pork pie type, but I use a plainer shortcrust.

Sieve the flour and salt into a basin. (Always sieve flour. Fresh air is a splendid ingredient). Rub in the margarine to the flour gently till the mixture looks like breadcrumbs, unless you have a mixer to do the job for you. Sprinkle on the water and lightly bring everything together. Transfer the pastry to a lightly floured board and, after just enough gentle kneading to make it manageable, roll, with a floured rolling pin, to the shape, but very slightly bigger than your dish. Dampen the edges of your pie-dish, cut narrow strips to lay on the edges, again dampen these and fold the pastry in two towards you, remembering to cut a small hole for the funnel to go through. Carefully lift the pastry into position and, with the knife handle leaning outwards a little, trim off the edges. If you take the first two fingers of your right-hand, with about an inch between them, then press the edges of the pie together, you can take the first finger of your left-hand, at the same time and pull the pastry up slightly. Continue this round the pie for an effective finish. Spare pieces of pastry, cut into leaves, can decorate the centre, kept in place with a drop of water.

While the oven is reaching its required heat of 400°, I suggest that you put the pie in the fridge, or on the cold slab in the larder to firm up. I bake my pie for 40 to 45 minutes, by which time the pastry should be cooked. If possible, use a pyrex glass pie dish, so that you can see what is happening to the meat. One very important point to always bear in mind, when re-heating meat, is to be certain that not only has the gravy and meat reached boiling point, but that it has remained at that stage for long enough for the heat to have penetrated right to the centre of the meat—the part you can't see. (I do this so well and thoroughly that I frequently have the gravy boil over the edge of the dish, and the confounded oven to clean as a result!).

To go back to the cold slab for a moment. Do you know that Mary, Queen of Scots, brought a slab of marble all the way from France to Edinburgh, to make sure her pastry cook made good pastry?

CHEESE STRAWS

Extra pieces of pastry left over? Splendid. Just gather them together, knead just enough to make it possible to roll out, grate on to this pastry some hard cheese, add a **tiny** sprinkling of cayenne pepper, fold the pastry into an oblong, then again into a square and roll out again. Now cut into fairly narrow strips, give each one a couple of twists and bake for a few minutes at 400°. Easy to make and very easy to eat.

POTTED MEAT

1lb (or more) **of the leanest shin of beef you can buy**
Enough water to barely cover the meat and to this add:

1 Tablespoon of vinegar (this is to soften the sinews)
Pepper
Salt
Nutmeg
A tiny scrap of bay leaf
Melted butter

Remove every scrap of fat and cut the meat into cubes of about one square inch. Add pepper, salt, bay leaf (if available). It is best cooked in an earthenware casserole, in the oven, and having put the meat into the casserole just barely cover it with the cold water and vinegar. Cook for three hours at 300° but check that it has not reached boiling point; should it do so reduce the heat to 250°. It must just simmer. Test that it is very tender. Cool, then put it through the mincer, using a coarse grinder first, then the finest one possible (twice if need be). The gravy will be sufficient to moisten it. Now add a little grated nutmeg, test for seasoning, put in small dishes and cover with melted butter.

Were you a victorian lady you would have netted, in fine cotton, little petticoats for the dishes, or crocheted them.

Have the potted meat on thin bread and butter, in sandwiches, on hot buttered toast, or do as I do, make a good batch, tuck it away in the freezer in little greaseproof packets inside a plastic bag—it won't be there long, I am sure.

SUMMER PUDDING

Fruit
Sugar
Water
Sliced white bread

Well butter a 2-pint size pyrex bowl. Take the crust off slices of white bread and line the inside of the bowl by simply sticking them to the butter (or margarine). Now stew about 1lb to 1½lbs of fruit, which can be raspberries, redcurrants or a mixture of fruits. The quantity of water added must, of necessity, depend on the juiciness of the fruit, and the sugar added must be to suit your own taste. The one important thing to remember

is that you must have it juicy—more juice than you would normally have for stewed fruit. When cooked spoon in the fruit and juice until the bowl is about half full, then add another layer of bread. Continue adding stewed fruit and juice until about 1 inch from the top, when the edges of the bread should be turned inwards, and another slice put across the middle, like a lid. In short, the whole of the fruit must be encased in bread. Reserve any extra fruit and juice. Now, stand the bowl inside another larger container, for it may overflow. Put a plate on top of the bread (a fraction smaller than the bowl), and on it put a weight, to press the whole affair overnight. Next day, looking through the glass, all the bread should be pink and well impregnated with fruit juice. If it is not, simply add that reserved fruit and juice. To serve, run a knife round the inside of the bowl, put a good deep serving bowl on top, and up-end the pudding! Serve with custard and, if possible, cream.

PLUM PUDDING

1lb suet
1lb sugar
1lb currants
1lb sultanas
8 eggs
¼ pint brandy (or milk)
1lb mixed peel
½lb plain flour
½lb bread crumbs
1 teaspoon salt
1 teaspoon mixed spice

Wash and dry fruits. Slice and chop finely the peel. Sieve flour. Mix together all the ingredients except the eggs and brandy. Beat eggs well, then add them, and stir in the brandy. Steam, in well greased bowls, for 13 hours. (You will know, of course, to have covered the bowls with well greased greaseproof paper, pleated in the middle to allow for rising, then to have put a second covering of pleated pudding cloths or foil).

When completely cold, fresh coverings should be put on and the puddings stored in a safe dry place. They will mature and improve for a year or more. Steam or boil for three to four hours on Christmas Day and serve with brandy sauce. Now for a safety measure! Serve the pudding with a sprig of arbutus stuck in the middle with one of its red berries; add a sprig of variegated holly on either side. This is to keep the witches away. It works! I've never seen a witch at my Christmas dinner table, though I won't vouch for what my guests may have seen.

PINEAPPLE PUDDING

1 tin pineapple
1½oz sugar
2ozs plain flour
2ozs butter
½ pint milk
2 large eggs

This is a very nice pudding to serve hot—equally good cold, but I doubt if you'll have any left for tomorrow.

Cut pineapple in small pieces and put in a pudding dish with some of the juice. Melt butter in a saucepan, stir in the flour (as if making a white sauce) and stir in the milk. Cook for five minutes. Stir in the sugar. When cool beat in the egg yolks and pour over the pineapple. Cook in

the oven for a few minutes while you beat the egg whites till very stiff. Pile the beaten whites on to the pudding, sprinkle with castor sugar and return dish to the oven to set the meringue.

If eaten cold, whipped cream giving the final touch, is gorgeous.

LEMON DELIGHT

1 teacup sugar (¼ pint)
1 teacup water
1 dessertspoon cornflour
1 large lemon
2 eggs

Separate the egg whites from the yolks (putting the whites into a good sized bowl as they will have to be whipped). Wash the lemon and add the fine rind to the yolks, mixing them together with a fork. Squeeze the lemon and mix the juice into the cornflour. Now put the sugar and water into a medium-sized saucepan and stir over gentle heat until the sugar is dissolved. Still stirring add the yolks and lemon rind, then the cornflour and lemon juice, to the mixture in the sauce pan, and cook for five minutes, just

boiling. (It will look like lemon curd). Turn the heat off and whisk the whites, preferably with a rotary beater, till very stiff. Gently fold in these whites to the mixture which will still have stayed hot in the pan. Serve cold. This quantity will make four generous helpings. I usually serve it in glass sundae dishes. (I have discovered, by chance, that the easiest way to get just the zest off the lemons, is to do so with a serrated edged knife—but **please** mind your fingers!).

COURTING CAKE

6oz plain flour
1 teaspoon baking powder
Pinch of Bi-carb
Pinch of salt
¼ lb butter (or soft margarine)
1 egg (beaten)
For filling use apricot, raspberry or strawberry
   jam.

Grease and line with greaseproof paper one 8in sandwich tin. (I usually take the precaution of adding a strip of foil, long enough to leave a piece at each end to make the finished cake more easily lifted out of the tin).

Cream butter and sugar thoroughly, add beaten egg, sift in flour, salt, baking powder and bi-carb.

Spread half the mixture in the tin, spread on a good layer of the chosen jam, then cover with the remaining mixture. Bake at 350° for 30 minutes, turn off heat but leave cake in oven for about five more minutes. The cake must be well cooked and evenly browned. As it is a very soft mixture let it cool in the tin, before lifting it carefully on to a cake rack to become a little firmer. Finally dredge it well with icing sugar. This is a delicious cake, whether one be courting or not.

BACHELOR CAKE

12ozs plain flour
Pinch of salt
1 teaspoon spice
1 teaspoon ground ginger
3ozs butter (or soft margarine)
12oz dried fruit (try to include some raisins)
8oz sugar
1 good tablespoon marmalade
1 good teaspoon bi-carb
Nearly 2 teacups milk
Blanched almonds for topping (not essential)

I bake this like gingerbread in a tin measuring 10in x 10in x 2in. It will completely fill this tin to the brim when cooked, so cut into quarters, each piece will slice into a useful shape. Well grease tin and, in addition, put a greased grease-proof paper on the base. Wash fruit and leave to drain. Into bowl sieve the flour, salt and spices. Rub in the fat, add the sugar, fruit, marmalade. Now mix the bi-carb into the first cup of milk and add to centre of ingredients. While mixing, add as much of the second cup as is required to make a dropping consistency. (This will depend on the size of that spoonful of marmalade, the size of your teacup and the type of flour). Beat the mixture very thoroughly before transferring to the tin. Scatter blanched almonds and bake at 325° for 40 minutes, reduce heat to 300° for 20 minutes (1 hour of baking in all). Turn off heat but leave in oven for 15 minutes. Remove from oven and allow another 15 minutes to cool in the tin before turning out. You will have noticed that there is no egg in this cake but you will not know it when you taste it. Also the fat content is low. Despite this, the taste is excellent.

WEDDING CAKE

10 eggs
18oz butter
2½lb currants
1¼lb powdered sugar
½lb candied lemon peel
¾lb citron peel
2oz almonds
1½lb plain flour
nutmeg to taste

For a three tier cake this quantity will have to be made twice. The first amount will fill a tin 10½ins. in diameter and 3½ins. deep. The second amount will be divided between an 8in tin and a 6in tin.

Make as many preparations as possible the day before the cake is to be baked. Line the tins with very well buttered greaseproofed paper, four layers of it. The side papers should be cut 3in deeper than the tins to allow for the bottom inch being folded over and snipped at intervals of an inch so that they can lie flat on the bottom of the tin, then the bottom layers laid on top. Cut double 'lids' of greased papers, 2in bigger than the size of the bottoms—these can then lie over the side papers, resting on the paper and preventing too much browning during the **six hours** baking which is to come.

Find the best possible currants, wash several times and leave overnight in a colander to drain. Cut the peel very thinly indeed. Blanch, skin and shred the almonds. Finally find a kind friend who will be prepared to stand by and hand you ingredients during the actual mixing.

An old-fashioned pottery bedroom wash-bowl is the best utensil in which to mix this cake and the best implements are your own hands, so, scrub up, as would a surgeon preparing for an operation. Have everything weighed, sieved if need be, the eggs separated and the whites well whisked—everything, including yourself, at room temperature. Warm the bowl and well dry it, put in the butter and start beating it with your hands. When creaming nicely, have your helper add the yolks slowly, keep on the beating, then, remembering the importance of the only raising agent, the air, incorporate the whites, then the sugar. By now you will have a beautifully creamy mixture into which add the fruit, etc. alternately with the flour. Remember the nutmeg. Check that everything has been included and transfer the mixture to the prepared tin, hollowing the centre very slightly to give a good flat cake when baked. Put on its little cover, transfer it to the middle of the oven, shut the door and don't open it again for six hours. Take a note of the time it has gone in and when it will be due to come out and either set the alarm clock or the timer, as an extra reminder—though I don't think you will forget.

I usually play for safety by leaving it in the tin to cool slightly before removing it from the tin.

The preparation for the two smaller cakes is exactly the same up to the point of putting the mixture into the tins. The easiest way of arriving at the correct amount for each tin is, I find, to stand them side by side and to try to get them to the same level in the tins. They should then come out at the same depth when cooked. Remember that slight hollow in the centre of the cake before cooking.

Timing is a little less easy with the smaller cakes. The temperature must still be as low, but the smaller cake will be ready soon and both will require a shorter time than the big one.

Don't be in a hurry to open the oven door, give time for them to have become quite firm and well brown. If a gentle touch with a finger allows the cake to spring back quickly it is time to test with a thin knitting needle. I said a gentle, quick touch—don't burn yourself, please. If the needle comes out of the centre of the tin with no vestige of cake adhering to it, I would say it is enough—as would a Victorian cook. If in doubt give it a little longer and test again.

I cooked three cakes, like these, on April 7th, 1935 for my wedding to be held four months later, on 17th August. They had matured wonderfully, wrapped in copious layers of greaseproof paper and well protected by tins with tight lids. They sat on a shelf of the dairy in the farm in Cheadle, North Staffordshire, where I was living, biding their time for the great day.

A week before they were to be appearing in all their glory each cake was cut through horizontally and given an inch thick layer of almond paste, then the tops and sides were wrapped in more almond paste. After a couple of days they each had two coats of royal icing, with a twenty-four hour rest between, then the final decoration. I decided on a simple cobweb-like design as a base, then sprays of pale pink roses and rose buds, made of marzipan, completed the job. Dare I say it? It was a very pretty cake and tasted as good as it looked.

SODA CAKE

1lb plain flour (I always sieve flour. Air is an excellent ingredient)
½lb butter
½lb granulated sugar
1lb currants (very well washed and dried)
¼lb candied peel
Mixed spice to taste
lemon rind and juice (and be generous)
1 teaspoon bi-carbonate of soda mixed in
Milk (? 12 fluid oz or more)
To be baked in a pretty hot oven an hour and three quarters.

That is the recipe as given in the old scrap-book. May I add my own findings? You will have noticed that there are no eggs in this cake, but you will not know it when you eat it. Remember that early tea-spoons were very big, also that we have no means of knowing the amount of liquid absorbed by flour in those times—for that matter present day flours vary greatly. Aim at what is known as a 'dropping' consistency—a spoonful of the mixture should just drop back into the bowl easily. I find a moderate oven gives best results—try 350°. The time will depend on the size of the tin.

Rub the butter into the sieved flour, be reasonably generous with the spice. Look for the plumpest currants you can find; I let them stand in water for a few moments after washing to help them to swell a little. Mix the bi-carb into part of the milk—you may not need as much as the recipe says. I like to bake this cake in a large tin, like gingerbread, and if you time the cooking to match lunch-time, part of the cake, cut in squares, and served with lemon sauce, vanilla sauce, or custard, goes down as a very acceptable pudding.

EXCELLENT SPONGE CAKE

On three quarters of a pound of sugar pour two-thirds of a teacup of water. Break 7 eggs into a deep earthen pan leaving out three of the whites. Boil the above sugar and water, pour it boiling hot upon the eggs. Whip them together a quarter of an hour with a whisk. Have ready half pound of fine flour well dried. Sift it very gently into the eggs. Add seven drops of the essence of lemon, whisking all the time. Have your mould ready buttered. Put your cake into a moderate oven immediately. You may ascertain when it is enough by putting in a skewer. When it comes out clean it is enough.

In Victorian days this sort of cake was never cut with a knife—the done thing was to tear it, with dainty fingers, into manageable sized pieces and then to serve it, with a glass of sherry wine or madeira after matins.

MERINGUES

3 egg whites
3ozs castor sugar
3ozs granulated sugar

I cook my meringues on the bottom of my largest cake tin, turned upside down. I do this because it is the smoothest and thickest tin I possess and it is easy to remove the finished meringues because there is no edge of the tin to get in the way of the pallette knife.

First put a tiny drop of oil on the tin, then with soft kitchen paper practically wipe it all off—you won't want to taste even the merest hint of oil.

Next have your oven at the lowest possible setting. The meringues are going to be dried rather than cooked. After three hours they are still to be as white as snow.

With a rotary whisk, whip those whites until you can turn the bowl upside down (for goodness sake do this over another bowl). Now add the granulated sugar and whip them back to the same firmness. With a metal tablespoon gently fold in the castor sugar as you shake it through a sieve. The whole point is to incorporate the maximum amount of air into the egg whites and, having got it there, to keep it there. Now take a damp spoon and a damp knife. Use the knife to slide the spoonful of meringue on to the tin and then to make the usual ridge shape along the top. Work from the centre of the tin outwards. Meringues can be piped, made small, large, put together in pairs with whipped, slightly sweetened cream between, or eaten plain. Try them with cream then, at the last moment pour hot chocolate sauce over the top—gorgeous! Some recipes say use all castor sugar but I prefer the texture resulting from this mixture of sugars. They will keep well in a tin (given half a chance) but without cream naturally. In my electric oven three hours at 200° is just right.

Try them with raspberries and cream. Make them tiny, in teaspoon size and built them up with whipped cream into a basket shape, on top of a sponge cake base, then fill with strawberries.

SHORTBREAD BISCUITS

8oz plain flour
5oz soft margarine
2oz granulated sugar
A little icing sugar

Sieve the flour. If you have a mixer put everything in it together and switch on at slow speed. Very quickly it will be gathering itself together. Stop!

Without a mixer, still put everything into a bowl together and with a fork press the margarine against the sides of the bowl. When the mixture begins to look like breadcrumbs take your hands to gather it together.

Now, with your hands, shape that shortbread heap into the shape of a shallow brick. **Don't** attempt to roll it out or be tempted to add extra flour. Take that brick and simply cut it into slices which will be about three inches long by one inch wide and roughly half an inch deep. Put them on to a greased tin, prick them with a fork, about four times each, and bake at 300° till very light fawn in colour. Just gently touch one and it should spring back to tell you that it wants to come out of the heat. Let them stand in the tin for a few minutes as they are very short

and must firm up a little. I find a fish slice the easiest means of lifting them on to a cake rack. When cold sprinkle generously with icing sugar. Keep in a tin.

OTHELLOS & DESDEMONAS

2½oz butter
5oz castor sugar
5oz plain flour
5 eggs

FILLING
2½oz butter
5oz castor sugar

Well butter small patty pans—or the shallow tins in which one would bake shallow jam tarts. Beat well the butter and sugar, then add, one by one, the yolks of three of the eggs. Beat whites of the five eggs till very stiff. Add sifted flour and the whites alternately. Bake in patty pans in dessertspoonfuls.

Beat filling to a cream and sandwich in pairs. Put in paper cases.

Over the Othellos drool chocolate glacé icing made with bitter chocolate, melted with a little warm water over a pan of hot water, then with icing sugar added till the back of a wooden spoon be easily coated.

Over the Desdemonas drool pink glacé icing with just a suggestion of vanilla (don't overdo the flavour).

SALAD DRESSING

2 eggs beaten till light
1 teaspoon salt
1 teaspoon mustard (dry)
1 tin condensed milk
1 cup vinegar

Beat the first four ingredients for several minutes. Stir in vinegar and stir well. Set aside to thicken. Keeps for weeks—given a chance.

LEMON CURD

5 eggs
1lb sugar
¼lb butter
Juice of 4 and rind of 3 lemons

Beat eggs just enough to make sure the whites and yolks are well mixed. Put all in a jar standing in boiling water and simmer for 2 hours. I like to stir it now and then.

ORANGE CURD

4 eggs
4 oranges
4oz butter
1lb sugar

Make in the same way as the lemon curd. A very good filling for an orange cake, made with the usual sponge sandwich cakes, and completed with an orange glacé icing.

MARROW, LEMON AND GINGER JAM

6lb marrow (peeled and cut into cubes)
¼ lb crystalized ginger, or 2ozs dried root ginger, or 3oz fresh ginger
6lb sugar
3 lemons

Approximate yield 10lb. This quantity would require an enormous pan. I would always make smaller batches. I am sure it sets better too. Boil the marrow till tender then mash well. I use the minimum amount of water. Started on low heat and well stirred the marrow soon provides its own cooking liquid and the less juice there is the shorter will be the cooking time of the jam. If the old hard type of root ginger has had to be used, then bruise it, put it in muslin and cook it with the marrow. To the mashed marrow add the grated rind and juice of the lemons, the grated fresh ginger (or the crystallized kind) and the sugar. Bring slowly to the boil allowing the sugar to dissolve, then stir and boil for about 20 minutes or till thick. Test on a cold plate in the usual way. Fresh ginger should be grated on a fine grater and any hard fibres discarded. The fresh flavour is very good indeed.

Bear in mind that marrow jam is not the best of keepers. I think it better to make smaller batches and to store the actual marrows for later use.

CRAB APPLE AND BRAMBLE JELLY

Crab apples or sour green apples (Wind falls, if sound, can be used)
Brambles (call them blackberries, if you like)
Sugar
Water

An equal weight of apple and brambles will make sure of a good setting jelly, though a better flavour will result from a larger proportion of brambles (up to twice the amount of brambles to apples, provided the brambles are firm and the apples really sour and green). Wash, remove stalks and any blemishes from the apples and cut up roughly. Put in pan and just cover with cold water. In a separate pan put the brambles which you have washed and looked over carefully. As these are very juicy fruits, add a little less water. Gently stew the fruits till really soft. The time will depend on the type and ripeness of the fruit. (If asked to share a pan with brambles, some apples end up looking like chamois leather gloves and refuse to 'fall'.) When soft, mash pulp well. I do this with a potato masher. Put both batches into a jelly bag and leave to drip. Don't be tempted to squeeze the bag to get extra juice—you'll end up with cloudy jelly if you do so. Measure the juice and to each pint allow 1lb of sugar.

In a **large** pan bring the juice to the boil, meanwhile slightly warming the sugar in a very cool oven. Stir in the sugar to the juice and keep the heat low, stirring all the time until all the sugar is dissolved. The heat may then be gradually increased to boiling point. **Care** is required. The boiling point of any sugar solution is much higher than that of boiling water; what is more, it readily rushes up the pan (hence the large pan). **Never** leave it. Should the phone or the door bell ring, let them ring until you have carefully turned off the heat and moved the pan off the heat. There are too many variables to give a length of time for this process —size of pan, quantity of jelly, setting quality of fruits, amount of heat, all have to be taken into account. When the quantity has reduced considerably lift the long handled wooden spoon and allow a little jelly to run back into the pan. When this begins to cling a little to the spoon test the jelly by putting a small amount on to a cold plate (not your Crown Derby). If when it cools it wrinkles as you tilt the plate, then carefully ladle it into warmed jars. You will be glad to stop the stirring, and beautiful jelly should be your reward.

All jellies are made in this way. Fruits vary in their pectin content so start on the easy ones, say redcurrant (lovely with lamb), gooseberry, apple (nice with a few cloves added), blackcurrant and mint jelly for which I give separate instructions.

MINT JELLY

Sour green apples
Mint
Vinegar
Sugar

This is specially good in winter—much nicer than mint sauce. Put in small attractive pots it could make small Christmas presents. Windfall apples are suitable, if sound, and I have even added the peelings of other apples when making this jelly.

To about 1lb of washed and cut up apples, add

a good handful of washed mint. Cover it with half vinegar, half water and slowly simmer it, as in previous recipe. Drip through jelly bag (or use an old teacloth tied over a small bowl—you will find it will stain). Measure the liquid and, as before, allow one pound of sugar to one pint of juice. Bring juice to boil, add sugar, boil to setting point but, before putting it into small warm jars, stir in a good tablespoonful of very well chopped mint and just **one** drop of green food colouring.

*   *   *

A note about **all** jams and jellies. Experience has taught me that the results are always better when small quantities are made. The very long boiling required for large quantities seems, to me, to spoil both colour and flavour.

BLACKCURRANT JAM

1lb Blackcurrants
1 pint water
2lb sugar

Wash and remove stalks from fruit. Boil the currants in water for ten minutes. Add warmed

sugar and, having kept the heat low until the sugar be dissolved, boil for ten minutes. Makes 4lb of excellent jam.

BRAMBLE MOULD

1lb jar bramble jelly
1 gill water
1 tablespoon corn flour
Lashings of whipped double cream

Make cornflour in gill of water. Add jelly and stir for twenty minutes with wooden spoon. Put in wet mould and turn out when set. Serve with cream. (Needless to say I would use a mixer in these days.) It is very good.

You will probably know brambles as blackberries, but I much prefer the prettier old name. They freeze very well (to come up to date for a moment). Just put them in plastic bags and they will taste wonderful, with apple in a tart, when the snow lies crisp and even. You may be able to pick the genuine wild kind, but modern agriculturists have a nasty habit of tidying up the hedges just before the fruit ripens. I play safe—grow my own. The thornless variety make the picking of the fruit less of a battle. They don't like lime but appreciate a well drained soil. They'll thank you for an ounce of sulphate of potash to the square yard in the winter, and an ounce of sulphate of ammonia to the square yard in March. In a good dry summer, stand them a good drink of water now and then, from June until they fruit. You won't have to wait till you go to Heaven for your reward. Loganberries enjoy the same routine. This 19th century fruit is said to have started off as a cross between a cultivated blackberry and a raspberry, a happy accident of nature.

MUSHROOM KETCHUP

Take the large caps of mushrooms gathered dry, and bruise them. Put some of them at the bottom of an earthen pan, strew some salt over, then mushrooms, then salt, till you have done. Boil the liquor, strain it through a thick flannel bag; to two quarts of liquor, put a large stick of horse-radish cut into small slips, five or six bay leaves, an onion stuck with twenty or thirty cloves, a quarter of an ounce each of mace, nutmeg, beaten allspice, black and white pepper, four or five ounces of ginger, and four ounces of shallots. Cover it close and simmer very gently till about one third is wasted. When it is cold bottle it and cork it close: in two months boil it up again, with a little more spice and a stick of horse-radish. It will keep the year which mushroom ketchup rarely does.

(I notice that there is no mention of vinegar. I would be tempted to add some although the large quantity of spices may make this superfluous.—K.I.)

PICKLED MUSHROOMS (Brown)

Rub small buttons with a bit of flannel and salt. Throw a little salt over and put them in a stew-pan with some mace and pepper; as the liquor comes out shake them well and keep them over a gentle fire till all of it be dried into them again. Put as much vinegar into the pan as will cover them, give it one warm, and turn all into a glass or stone jar. They will keep two years and are delicious.

PICKLED WALNUTS

Green walnuts
Brine
Spiced vinegar

Green walnuts are said to be ready for pickling early in July but, as the age of the tree, the area and the soil may vary, I would always seek local advice. The essential point is that the shell should not have started to develop. As this begins at the opposite end from the stalk it can be detected by testing it with a darning needle, thrust into the nut. If all is well, prepare the brine by adding ¼lb of cooking salt to one quart of boiling water and leaving it to get cold. (The amount of brine will depend on the quantity of nuts). Bear in mind that walnut stain is difficult to remove. You may like to wear gloves. Wipe the nuts then prick them with a fork, put into a large container and cover with brine. They should be allowed to soak for about two weeks but, during this time, strain off the brine and replace it with fresh brine twice.

Now drain them, spread on big flat dishes in the sun to become black, turning them when need be. This will take about a day. Pack in jars and cover with hot spiced vinegar.

Spiced vinegar. To one quart of malt vinegar add 1oz mixed pickling spices, readily obtainable from a grocer, or you can make up your own mixture of black peppercorns, allspice, whole root ginger, a few cloves, mace. (If you are inexperienced I'd be inclined to settle for the ready mixed). Also add ½ teaspoonful salt. Bring to the boil. Allow to stand for a time to extract the flavour of the spices then strain.

Bring back to the boil, the strained vinegar, and pour it **hot** on to the walnuts. When **completely** cold cover the jars carefully with parchment paper or lids specially prepared for pickles. Not, under any circumstances, should vinegar be allowed to come in contact with metal. Keep for at least a month before use—or longer. The amount of vinegar required will, of course, depend on the quantity of walnuts, but be sure to more than cover the nuts; however carefully covered there is always a risk of evaporation.

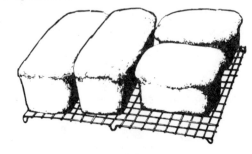

SPICES AND HERBS

Thoughts on some of the flavourings, spices and herbs which I find of use, might be helpful. Top of my list would always come discretion. It's the subtle flavour, which can't quite be placed which makes your friend say, "Yes, please, I'd love some more".

Spices first:- Red for danger where **cayenne pepper** is concerned, it is very hot indeed. **Black pepper**, freshly ground, is always to be preferred to white, to my taste. Prepared **mustard** is useful but give me it freshly mixed, just with water, please. **Cinnamon, mixed spice** and **ground ginger**, a little of each gives a good flavour for cakes. **Stick cinnamon** is splendid for pickles and now that one can buy fresh **root ginger** there's nothing to equal it in things like marrow ginger jam (and I use it, finely grated, in gingerbread too). Buy whole **nutmegs** every time, the ground variety never tastes so good. **Paprika**, though red in colour, is not hot. It is delicious in company with tomatoes and many fish dishes. Mixed whole pickling spices are useful for things like pickled onions and red cabbage. **Cloves** are a must (used with discretion) and **mace**, the outer coat of the nutmeg, has a gentle flavour which blends well with beef—in potted beef for example—and often turns up in pickles and chutneys. **Curry powder** has its moments though the gourmet will mix his or her own. **Turmeric** for piccalilli and **saffron** for saffron cakes.

Nothing can equal fresh herbs, growing near the back door where I have **mint, parsley, chives, sage, lemon thyme** (much nicer than ordinary thyme), **marjoram, rosemary** (sometimes a little difficult) and **basil**, which will grow easily from seed and is specially good with tomatoes. Many of these could be grown on the kitchen window-ledge—just ask the nurseryman. I like to dry a few which vanish in the winter, like **mint**. Picked when young, washed, hung in bunches in the garden from the clothes line to dry a little, then hung indoors inside a paper bag until crisp, mint can be rubbed through a fine sieve, kept in a small glass screw-topped jar, and pea soup can be transformed in the winter. Just cook a chopped onion in stock (a stock cube will do), add frozen peas, a pinch of sugar to give the 'garden fresh' image to the peas and finally sprinkle on the mint. (If a stock cube has been used no further seasoning will be required). Try it! **Bay leaves** are a must to me. They can be bought dried unless you have a tree or, like me, a kind friend. The same friend grows **celeriac** and, when she brings me some, I always dry the leaves, in the same way as the mint, whereby I have a very concentrated celery flavour to add to soups or stews.

GINGER WINE

To one gallon of water 4lb of coarse brown sugar, three ounces of the best ginger, 2 lemons. Boil it for a short time till the sugar be properly mixed. When cool put a slice of toasted bread with a little yeast on it. Put it in a barrel for two months and then bottle it.

After that, what? Take cover, I suggest.

ELDER WINE

One quart of berries to be added to one quart of water, boil half an hour, run the liquor and break the fruit through a hair sieve. Then to every quart of juice add one pound of sugar. Boil the whole for a quarter of an hour with some Jamaica pepper, ginger and a few cloves. Pour it into a bowl and put yeast to it when of a proper warmth. To stand in the wart three days then to be bottled into large bottles for six months. It will then be ready for bottling into glass bottles, when a little rum should be added to it.

SLOE GIN

1 quart sloes (some of which must be pricked)
1lb loaf sugar
2 quarts best London Gin

Sloes may be expected to be ripening in late August. Put the gin into bottles and keep for six months before using. The bottles should be shaken occasionally. I have tasted this and very good it is.

2. *Favourite Country Recipes*

A selection from Dalesman readers

Favourite Country Recipes

A selection from Dalesman readers

The first six recipes are illustrated on pages 41-46

ROAST DUCKLING
Fig. 1

1 Duckling (approximately 5lb)
1lb cooking apples
1 x 8oz can cranberry sauce

Defrost duckling as directed. Wash well then rub a little salt into the skin. Peel and core apples and cut into fairly thick slices. Put into bowl, combine well with cranberry sauce and pack into duckling. Roast exactly as directed on the wrapper for the length of time recommended. Serves 4.

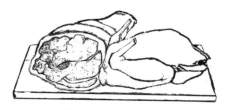

MEAT BALLS
Fig. 2

8oz chuck steak
8oz pork fillet
1 large onion
4oz fresh white breadcrumbs
8 fl oz bottle soda water
1 egg, beaten
Salt and pepper
2oz butter
2 tablespoons oil

Pass steak, pork and onion twice through fine blade of mincer. Add breadcrumbs and beat in soda water and beaten egg. Add seasoning, cover and chill for 1 hour.

Shape mixture into 8 oblongs, 4in x 2in x ¾in thick. Heat butter and oil together in large frying pan and fry meat balls until browned, 6 - 8 minutes on each side. Drain. Serves 4.

DUMPLING TOPPERS

Fig. 3

4oz self-raising flour
1 level teaspoon grated lemon rind
2oz finely shredded suet (or 1oz butter)
about 3 tablespoons cold water
squeeze of lemon juice

These recipes are useful to keep as a reference for any time when casseroles are on the menu—and especially so when vegetables are expensive and scarce.

Mix ingredients to a firm dough. Roll into 6 or 8 balls. Place on top of nearly cooked meat and vegetables (do not submerge in liquid) in casserole. Cover and cook about 30 minutes in a moderately hot oven.

Bacon Dumplings: Sift ½ level teaspoon dry mustard and sprinkling pepper with flour and add 1 tablespoon chopped cooked bacon or ham to above.

Spiced Apple Dumplings: Add 2 heaped tablespoons finely chopped apple, 1 tablespoon chopped onion and a grating of nutmeg. Especially good with casserole of liver or pork.

PEACH MELBA CAKES

Fig. 4

3oz butter or margarine
3oz caster sugar
2 eggs
6oz self-raising flour, sieved
3 tablespoons milk
FILLING AND TOPPING:
3 individual vanilla-flavoured ice cream blocks
    (the larger size)
raspberry jam or bramble jelly
1 medium can peach slices, drained

Cream fat and sugar till light and fluffy then beat in the eggs, one at a time. Stir in flour alternately with the milk then turn mixture into a well-greased shallow tin, approximately 11½ inches by 7½ inches. Bake towards the top of the oven at 380°F or gas Mark 5 for 15 to 20 minutes. Turn out and cool on a wire tray.

When the cake is cold, trim away crisp edges then cut up into 12 equal-sized pieces. Spread tops of 6 with jam then decorate each with 3 peach slices. Split each ice cream block in half lengthwise, put on to the remaining 6 pieces of cake then cover with those already prepared. Serve at once.

CRANBERRY AND APPLE MOUSSE

Fig. 5

2 x 8oz cans cranberry sauce
12oz apples, weighed after peeling and coring
4 tablespoons cold water
2 envelopes (6 teaspoons) gelatine
¼ pint boiling water
2 egg yolks
3 level tablespoons caster sugar
¼ pint double cream
2 egg whites

Prepare dish first. Put a collar - or strip - of folded greaseproof paper round a 1½ to 2 pint sized straight sided dish, making sure paper stands at least 1½-inches above top edge. Hold in place with sticky tape then lightly brush inside of paper with salad oil.

Open cans of cranberry sauce and reserve 2 tablespoons for decoration. Slice apples thinly, put into a pan with cold water, cover with lid and simmer gently until soft. Meanwhile shower gelatine into boiling water and stir briskly until dissolved. Beat cooked apples with a fork or whisk until smooth and purée-like then stir in egg yolks, sugar, cranberry sauce, dissolved gelatine and half the cream. Leave until cold and just beginning to thicken and set. Whisk egg whites to a stiff snow then, using a large metal spoon, fold cranberry mixture into them. Transfer to prepared dish and chill for at least 2 hours or until mousse is firm and set. Remove paper then decorate by piping small rings of cream on the top and then filling each "nest" with reserved cranberry sauce. Serves 8.

ROLL-BURGER PICNIC

Fig. 6

For hungry youngsters there's nothing better than a burger picnic. Meatburgers are easy to make—just seasoned minced steak, shaped into cakes and grilled about 5 minutes each side. When they are quite cold (and this is important) slip them into soft buttered baps or crusty fresh wholemeal or white rolls—or between buttered slices of fresh French or Vienna bread.

For an 'after' choose little fruit pies or easy-to-pack-and-carry apple slices made at home or bought at the pastrycook's. Pack crisp and juicy salad pick-ups, favourite ones, for the burgers, and fruit to finish the meal.

1. DUCKLING WITH CRANBERRIES

2 (left). MEAT BALLS
3 (right). DUMPLING
           TOPPERS

4 (left).   PEACH MELBA
            CAKES
5 (right). CRANBERRY AND
            APPLE MOUSSE

6 (left).   SUMMER PICNICS
7 (right). CHRISTMAS
           BISCUITS

8. CHRISTMAS
    PASTRIES

UPSIDE-DOWN PIE

½lb tomatoes
¼lb minced meat
1 large onion
Teaspoon of meat extract
1 tablespoon of water
Pepper and Salt to taste
Short Pastry

Slice tomatoes and put in bottom of well greased sandwich tin. Mix meat, finely chopped onion and seasoning together and place on top of the tomatoes. Cover with the pastry. Bake in a moderately hot oven for 45 minutes, turn out on to a dish and serve with gravy and vegetables.

Mrs Tuck

YORKSHIREMAN'S GOOSE

½lb beef liver
1 onion
1lb potatoes
1 teaspoonful flour
½ teaspoonful pounded sage
Salt
Pepper

Wash, wipe and slice liver. Put the flour on a plate, season liver with salt and pepper and dip it in the flour. Place the slices in layers in a greased dish. Parboil the onion, mince it, mix it with the sage, and sprinkle between the layers of liver, pouring in sufficient stock (or water) to come half-way up the dish.

Parboil the potatoes, cut them in slices, place them over the top of liver to form a crust, and bake for an hour until the top potatoes are nicely browned. This will be found to be a most appetising and tasty dish.

Mrs M. Winskill

CREOLE EGGS

3 eggs
6oz tomatoes
2 level dessertspoonsful chopped onions
¾ - 1oz rice
2 rashers of bacon
5 level dessertspoonsful grated cheese
Seasoning to taste
Brown bread and butter

Wash the rice and cook it in boiling water. When tender turn into a strainer to drain. Cut the rind from the bacon, then cut into small pieces. Put into frying pan and cook until tender, then cook the onion in the bacon fat. Skin and chop the tomatoes then add to the bacon and onion and cook altogether. Add rice and seasoning.

Grease three individual glasses (fire-proof) and divide the mixture equally between them. Break each egg into a cup, then tip one into each glass and sprinkle with grated cheese over the egg yolk. Bake in a very moderate oven until the white of the egg is set. Serve with thin slices of brown bread and butter.

Mrs Ivy Simpson

YORKSHIRE PUDDING

Typical Yorkshire pudding is made with milk in order to obtain lightness and crispness, and it is intended that there should be no fat in the mixture. Originally, it was served with thick gravy, as an extra course before the main course, but is now often served with the roast beef.

4oz flour
1 teaspoon salt
¼ pint milk
¼ pint water
1 egg

Break the egg into the flour and salt previously mixed in a basin. Add enough liquid to make a beating consistency. Beat well and leave to stand for half an hour. Heat the oven to 450 degrees. For small puddings use 2½in by 1in size bun tray and put a knob of fat in each tin. Place the tray in the oven until the fat is smoking hot. In the meantime add the rest of the liquid to make a batter. Take the tray from the oven and put two tablespoons of the batter in each tin. Bake for fifteen to twenty minutes.

Jean Dawson

APPLE PIE

Here are some ways of getting variation into one of our favourite traditional dishes:-

1. Addition of a few seedless raisins, with or without snippings of orange peel. Remove all white pith before cutting up peel.
2. By adding one or two cloves.
3. Scattering, after cutting out heel, a few dark red rose petals, the old fashioned sweet smelling ones, on top of apples before putting on the pastry lid.
4. A squeeze of lemon juice and grater of lemon peel. Besides imparting a delicious flavour the lemon helps to keep the apples a good colour.
5. A sprinkling of ground ginger brightens up a tasteless variety of apples.
6. Instead of adding water to apples in pie-dish, in readiness for covering with pastry, use a few spoonsful of beer or cider. When a tart is wanted for a celebration meal try adding a little rum.
7. An old fashioned custom, which I well remember being practised by an aunt. When a pie was brought to the table hot, a wedge of crust was cut out and before serving a nut of butter (margarine can now be used) stirred in among the hot apples.

Most of these suggestions can also be brought into play in making boiled apple puddings. It would be interesting to know if any readers can offer other suggestions.

Doris Wood

CHEESE CURD TART

1½ pints of milk
1 teaspoonful of rennet
2 eggs
4oz sugar
4oz butter
    (or half butter and half margarine)
4oz currants
1 saltspoon grated nutmeg

Warm milk slightly, add rennet and stir. Let it stand for 15 minutes, then stir with a fork. Pour off the whey until only curd is left. Cream butter and sugar together. Add eggs well beaten. Add curd and stir. Add currants and nutmeg. Line pastry cases with pastry and put the mixture in. A taste of rum can be added if liked. Heat oven at pastry heat.

M.E. Bell

YORKSHIRE PARKIN

12oz medium oats
4½oz flour
4½oz sugar
8oz treacle
6oz lard or margarine
¼oz ginger
5oz milk

Mix the dry ingredients in a bowl, melt the treacle and fat together and mix into the other ingredients. Add the milk and mix well. Put into a tin lined with greaseproof paper and bake in a slow oven—about 1½ hours for the above quantity.

It is best to keep it for a week or more before eating it. I use stone-ground wholemeal flour, black treacle and brown sugar (known as 'pieces'). This gives a rich nutty flavour. If a sweeter product is required white sugar and golden syrup can be used or any mixture of these. Some people prefer a stickier and moister product and a little more milk can be used and the parkin cooked more quickly.

John E. Scott

CLAP BREAD

½lb oatmeal
¼lb flour
pinch of carbonate soda
pinch of salt
small quantity of fat

Mix flour and oatmeal and other dry ingredients. Rub in fat until it feels brittle. Mix with cold water. Roll out thin, cut into shapes and bake.

Mrs J. Walton

HAVERCAKE

1 pint of milk
8oz butter
1lb oatmeal
1 tablespoon sugar
3 teaspoons baking powder
8oz flour

Boil the milk and pour it over the oatmeal. Stir well, add the butter and sugar and then stir in the flour and baking powder. Knead the

dough well, roll thin on a floured board and then cut out the biscuits. Bake till light brown in a moderate oven.

George Norman

LOAF CAKE

2 breakfast cups flour
1 cup raisins
1 cup currants or sultanas
¾ cup of sugar
2oz margarine
1 teaspoon baking powder
1 teaspoon carbonate of soda
1 cup water

Mix soda and baking powder with flour and rub in margarine. Put the fruit into a pan with water and bring to the boil. When cold mix all together. Bake for 1½ hours in a moderate oven.

Miss Crisp

SPICE CAKE

The baking of the 'spice cake' was quite an event —a special day in our household. The loaves were baked in the ordinary bread tins, and the big baking bowl, shiny yellow inside, used for the weekly mixing of the bread dough, was brought into use for the mixing of the 'spice cake', for mother's recipe, handed down in the family, began: 'Take a half-stone flour, three and a half pounds butter, four pounds sugar, four pounds currants, etc.'

Does anyone make this quantity today I wonder? Spice loaf was not as rich as Christmas cake, so the butter was rubbed into the flour, then all the dry ingredients mixed together. From then on was a busy day for mother. She kept two ovens going—one gas, one fire. Dry mixture was measured by pints into a mixing bowl, the necessary eggs and milk added, and the mixture then transferred to four loaf tins, which were put into one oven. This process was repeated throughout the day, with four loaves in each batch, both ovens being kept in use. When we came home in the evening there would be the lovely sight of about forty shiny, brown, deliciously smelling spice loaves, and what pleased us more, a tasting cake. This was the last of the mixture, made into a big flat cake on a baking sheet instead of in a loaf tin, and this we could sample straight away. The loaves when cold were stored in tins, and what a number were needed!

Nearer Christmas, any and every caller was offered spice cake, cheese, and a glass of ginger wine, or a cup of tea, with the invitation to have 'a happy month.' As many count each mince pie, eaten in a different home, as 'a happy month' in the coming year, so we counted 'happy months' by different tastes of 'spice cake'.

Louise E. Thornton

PEPPER CAKE

1½lb flour
½lb moist brown sugar
1 teaspoon pearl ash, melted in a little milk
1oz powdered cloves
1½lb treacle
5 well beaten eggs

Pepper Cake is a form of gingerbread given to children when they went around to people's houses at Christmas.

Mix all ingredients well together with well beaten eggs. Bake in moderate oven for two hours.

A. Driver

DOCK PUDDING

'In the spring a young man's fancy turns to thoughts of love.' This may be true of some men —but my husband has another love for which he yearns ere the first notes of the thrush are heard: dock pudding. At the first sign of spring, as the first new blades of grass make their appearance, he will say, 'It's time we were going docking, I'm sure they'll be ready by now.'

No bloodhounds ever followed the trail more diligently than we did up hill and down dale. In the end, just as we were beginning to think we should have to go home with our bags empty, we would see a lovely green patch of docks in the next field corner. No eagle every swooped down on its prey more quickly than we did and in a few minutes we had filled our bags. Now, after years of experience, believe me, we know all the best dock fields for miles around.

Having got our docks, however, another

essential ingredient to a really good dock pudding is a few nettles, so it is as well, in searching for docks, to keep a close look-out for these too. Any novices who happen to be with us and are chary of gathering these vicious plants are always told 'They don't sting this month,' or 'squeeze them hard as you pluck them and they won't sting.' Needless to say our advice is not gratefully received.

The next thing to do having gathered our docks and nettles, is to get home as quickly as possible to start the long business of picking, washing, and chopping them—that is, if you want to be in bed by midnight. However, after I have washed and picked them, I have found that a good way is to put them through a mincer —thus ensuring that they are all pulped evenly— and also so that they do not take as long to boil.

Put the minced docks and nettles in a pan with a little water, salt and pepper, and a few chopped spring onions. Boil for about twenty minutes then add a little oatmeal and boil again for a few minutes. Turn out into a basin and by this time it will probably look like something else found in the fields! Don't be put off by appearances however; put some in a frying pan with a nice piece of streaky bacon, and in a few minutes you will be enjoying (I hope) a delicious meal.

Mrs Phyllis Stainton

FARMHOUSE GIRDLE CAKE

¾lb flour
2oz ground rice
2oz sugar
1oz lard
3oz currants
1 teaspoonful salt
2 teaspoonsful baking powder
1 gill liquid—half milk and half cream

Mix flour, ground rice, salt, sugar and baking powder. Rub in lard. Mix in currants which have been previously washed and dried. Then add the liquid and mix to a moderately soft dough. Roll this out to a ¼ inch thickness. Prick all over with a fork and bake in a fairly hot girdle until nicely browned on both sides. It can be cut in halves or quarters for convenience in turning. This cake is delicious split and buttered and eaten hot.

Muriel Gaudern

ROWAN JELLY

I have always liked experimenting with cookery, and when I came across an old recipe for Rowan Jelly, just at a time when the fell-side was ablaze with scarlet bushes, I felt that I must try it. According to the recipe, this jelly was the correct thing to serve with grouse; we did not own any shooting, but it would do to use instead of redcurrant jelly.

The trouble with these old recipes is that they do not give clear measurements; they say, 'Take some', which is rather vague. My first attempt was as bitter as gall. I tried again, and got it a little better, but I made several attempts before I got it to my liking, and then it was a great success. It was a lovely colour—rich, bright vermilion. Here is the recipe:

2lbs berries (stalked)
2lbs apples cut up, but not peeled nor cored
juice and rind of one lemon
1 teaspoonful of cloves

Cover with water, boil to a pulp, strain through a bag all night, boil up to a jelly next day, allowing one pound of sugar to each pint of juice. Pot and cover, and leave for a month before using.

Norah Sturgeon

SAMPHIRE PICKLE

Well wash the sand from the samphire and put into a pan, cover with water. Boil until tender. It doesn't take long. Boil about one pint of vinegar with ¼oz of 'pickling spice' tied in muslin and let it go cold. Well drain the samphire, and when cold put into a jar and cover with cold vinegar. It is ready for eating in a few days.

The way to eat samphire is to hold it by the stalk and draw off the tender part in the mouth, just like eating asparagus. In fact, it tastes much the same before adding the vinegar.

Mrs A. Eastham

BEE WINE

Place one dessertspoonful of granulated sugar, and one dessertspoonful of syrup into a large jug and pour over it one pint of hot (not boiling) water. Stir well until dissolved. When cool pour it on to the "bees" or yeast in a large glass jar. Add root ginger, then strain off liquid every three weeks when the process may be repeated.

Dissolve 4oz sugar and 4oz treacle (not syrup) in 1½ pints of water. Put in a few pieces of the 'ginger beer plant' (saccharomyces pyriformis), and each day add about one teaspoonful of sugar. This sets up brisk fermentation, so that on the following day a portion of the fermented liquid may be filtered off and drunk. The length of fermentation and the amount of sugar determines the potency, but the liquid should be maintained at 1½ pints.

K. R. Cass

MANGOLD ALE

Mangolds grow well in the Dales. About 10lb of roots to a gallon of water is considered an ordinary mixture, but a better quality can be made by using 15lb. It can be sweetened with treacle. Here is the way.

Clean and mash the roots, taking off the tops and paring away the rind, then boil until soft and pulpy. Squeeze the liquor from the pulp, and then boil it again with about six ounces of hops to every nine gallons of liquor. Afterwards work with yeast in the usual way.

The result is a potent and stimulating brew,

K. Herd

3. *Farmhouse Cooking*

Meat Dishes and Savouries

CHEESE SOUFFLE

3 eggs
3oz cheese
1oz margarine
½ oz flour
1 gill milk
Salt
Pepper
Mustard

Melt margarine, add flour and cook until bubbly. Add the milk and stir over a low flame until the mixture leaves the sides of the saucepan. Add the grated cheese, salt, pepper and mustard to taste. Remove the pan from the gas and stir in the lightly beaten yolks of eggs. Whip the whites of the eggs very stiffly and fold in lightly. Put in greased and warmed souffle dish and bake 20 to 30 minutes in moderate oven. Sufficient for 3 or 4 people.

BLACK PUDDING

1 quart of blood
1 quart of milk
2 cupsful breadcrumbs
1 cupful oats
1lb leaf fat not rendered
1 tablespoonful salt
1 tablespoonful mint
1 teaspoonful pepper
1 teaspoonful marjoram
1 teaspoonful thyme
1 cup rice boiled in 3 cups of water

Boil rice, draw to side and leave until all water is absorbed. Strain blood and place in bowl with rice, oats, milk, crumbs, fat and seasoning. Mix well together. Bake a little in dish in oven, taste and add more seasoning if required. Barley may be used instead of rice.

BEAN PIE

1lb haricot beans soaked overnight, cooked and
  salt added
1lb onions finely chopped and cooked, adding
sage ½ teaspoonful

Arrange onions in the bottom of a pie dish.
Cover with the beans then cover with slices of
tomato. Cover the whole with pastry and bake in
a hot oven. Failing tomatoes mix the beans
with a generous helping of tomato sauce. Serve
with Marmite gravy.

POTATO PANCAKES

2 large potatoes
2 medium onions
2 tablespoonsful flour
2 eggs
A little celery salt
Dash of cayenne pepper

Grate potatoes and onions into a basin—add
flour and seasoning and mix the eggs into a soft

paste. Heat some olive oil in frying pan and drop
a tablespoonful of the mixture into the pan.
Turn when brown underneath. Serve with
tomato sauce or cranberry sauce whichever is
preferred.

CORNISH PASTIES

4oz minced beef
2oz grated raw potato
A little grated onion
Pepper and salt to taste

Make ½lb of very short pastry (puff pastry is
best). Roll out and cut into 6 rounds with a
saucer. Put a spoonful of the meat mixture into
the centre of each, press the edges and trim off.
Brush over with beaten egg. Make 3 slanting cuts
across the top with a knife. Place on greased
baking sheet and bake in a hot oven about
30 minutes.

Apple and
omato.
utney

Raspberry
Jam
1966

SAUSAGE ROLLS

½lb of very short pastry. Roll out and cut into
  pieces about 4 inches square.
Use ½lb of sausage meat and divide into 10 or
  12 portions

Roll the meat (in the hands well floured) and lay
it on the pieces of pastry. Fold the pastry over
with a slight overlap. Place on greased baking
sheet with overlap underneath. Brush over with
beaten egg. Cut across top with knife 2 or 3
slanting cuts about an inch long. Bake in hot
oven until nicely brown—about 20 minutes.

POTATO JANE

1lb potatoes
1 or 2oz breadcrumbs or oatmeal
½ onion
2 or 3oz grated cheese
1 carrot
¼ pint milk and water
Seasoning

Prepare the vegetables, slice potatoes, carrot,
onion, and grated cheese. Grease fireproof dish,
put vegetables in the dish in layers, seasoning
each layer (potatoes, carrot, onions, breadcrumbs, cheese). Finish with layer of potatoes
and put mixed breadcrumbs and cheese on top
of these. Pour over milk and water. Bake in a
moderate oven for 1 to 1½ hours.

BEEF STEAK PUDDING

1½lbs beef steak
1 kidney
Pepper and salt

Cut the steak and kidney into small pieces. Make
a batter of 6ozs flour, 2 eggs, not quite 1 pint
milk. Pour a little batter in bottom of pie dish,
then put steak and kidney in with one pint water.
Pour remainder of batter on and bake 1½
hours.

SAVOURY PUDDING

8oz breadcrumbs, soak for one hour in water
3oz suet
1 large onion
2 tablespoonsful oatmeal or quaker oats
1 teaspoonful herbs
Salt and pepper
1 teacupful milk added the last

Put 1oz of dripping in tin, allow to heat until blue smoke appears. Put in mixture and bake about 1 hour.

STUFFED TOMATOES

3 tomatoes
1½ tablespoonsful fresh breadcrumbs
½ tablespoonful chopped ham and bacon
Small piece onion finely chopped
½oz butter or margarine
½ teaspoonful chopped parsley
Seasoning

Wipe tomatoes and cut a small round from each tomato at end opposite from stalk. Scoop out the centre with teaspoon handle. Fry onion in batter, add bacon or ham and cook. Add rest of ingredients with sufficient tomato pulp to bind. Fill the tomatoes with mixture and pile neatly on top. Bake in a moderate oven for about 15 minutes. Sprinkle with a little grated cheese. Replace lids and serve on toasted or fried bread and garnish with parsley.

BEEF MOULD

1lb beef
1lb ham
½lb breadcrumbs
2 eggs
Nutmeg
Pepper and salt

Mince through the machine and mix with ½lb breadcrumbs, nutmeg, pepper and salt to taste. Mix in two eggs, place in greased mould and boil for 2½ hours.

YORKSHIRE GOOSE PIE

Split a large goose down the back and take out all the bones. Prepare a couple of ducks and a turkey in the same way. Lay the goose on a clean table with the breast down and lay the turkey into the goose in the same manner, have ready a large hare well cleaned, and cut in pieces and stewed in the oven with a pound of butter, a quarter of an ounce of mace beat fine, the same of white pepper and salt to your taste. Stew it till the meat leaves the bones; and skim the butter off the gravy. Pick the meat clean off, and beat it very fine in a marble mortar with the butter you have taken off the goose, and then lay it in the turkey.

Take 24 pounds of the finest flour, 6lbs of butter and ½lb rendered suet. Raise the pie in an oval form, and make the crust very thick, roll a piece of paste very thin, and cut it into shapes of leaves or flowers. Rub the yolks of eggs over the wall of the pie, lay the ornaments upon them, and put yolks of eggs over them. Then turn the goose etc. upside-down, and lay them in the pie with the ducks at each end, and six woodcocks (boned) laid at the sides.

Then roll your lid pretty thick and lay it on; you may ornament the lid in any way you please, but make a hole in the middle of it, and make the walls of your pie an inch and a half higher than the lid, then rub it all over with the yolks of eggs, and bind it round with three-fold paper, and lay the same on the lid.

Bake it four hours, and when it comes out of the oven, melt two pounds of butter in the gravy that comes from the hare, and pour it hot into the pie through a tun-dish. Close it well up and do not cut it in less than a week. If your pie is to be sent any distance, stop up the hole in the middle of the lid with cold butter.

—from a cookery book dated 1841, quoted
by a Darlington reader

ONION TOAST

Spanish onions
Cheese
Hot buttered toast
Mustard
Salt and pepper

Fry some sliced Spanish onions a nice brown and spread thickly over rounds of hot buttered toast. Season. Cover with thin slices of cheese spread with a little mustard. Put into a hot oven or before a fire until the cheese is melted. Serve at once.

STEAK CASSEROLE

1 piece steak 2 inches thick
1 tablespoonful dripping
2 medium sliced onions
4 small diced carrots
1 tin tomato soup
Potatoes as required
Salt, pepper and celery salt

Season steak with salt and pepper and pound a little flour into steak. Heat the dripping and sear the steak in the hot fat until brown. Place steak in a casserole, pour a tin of tomato soup over meat and simmer gently for an hour. Then cover meat with sliced onions, potatoes and carrots and cook another hour. Remove meat and vegetables, thicken gravy and serve.

SAVOURY MEAT ROLL

4oz short pastry
4oz minced beef
Shredded onion and carrot
Blade of mace
Pepper and salt

Roll out pastry and spread mixture of meat and vegetables over two-thirds of pastry. Damp the edges, roll up and press into shape. Bake in a moderately hot oven for 30 minutes. Serve with thick gravy and a dressed vegetable.

SAUSAGE SAVOURY

8 sausages
4 tomatoes medium size
½ breakfast cup of breadcrumbs
1 breakfast cup of gravy

Grease a fireproof dish and put a layer of sliced tomatoes in the bottom, skin the sausage and place them next in the dish, then a layer of tomatoes, topping with the breadcrumbs. Pour gravy over all and, if liked, sprinkle a little sage on the top. Bake in a hot oven 450 degrees F. for half an hour.

SAUSAGE MOULD

1lb sausage meat
2oz cheese
1 small grated onion
1 level teaspoonful sage

Mix sausage meat and sage together with finely grated cheese and onion. Put into greased dish and bake or steam for 1 hour. Eat hot or cold with salad.

4. *Christmas Recipes*

by Anne R. Burkett

Christmas Recipes

by Anne R. Burkett

CHRISTMAS EVE—darkness, shadows thrown by lit candles, the scents of holly, ivy, laurel and fir, and a meal of 'furmenty', yule cakes and cheese. I am in my fifties now, and this has been part of my life all these years and back further still for generations. Is the custom still kept up in the Dales? From Coventry to Leeds, out to Australia, in Cumbria, and now again in Coventry I have never met anyone who knew of it.

The tradition has come to me from my Yorkshire ancestors, William Manby, a wine-merchant of Knaresborough, who married Margaret (Peggy) Benson, heiress of Halton East between Skipton and Bolton Abbey. Their son, the Rev Aaron Manby, vicar of Nidd, married Harriet Tooke. Their son, another Aaron, was my great-grandfather and also entered the Church and took over from his father as vicar of Nidd. He married Henrietta Lewis (a visitor to Yorkshire where her brother was for a time vicar of Ripon). They lived at York House, Farnham, where my grandmother spent her early years, but the family moved south for health reasons and my grandmother married a Devonian. My mother grew up in the south and nowhere was the influence more strongly felt than in the Christmas traditions and recipes—or 'receipts' as they were then called.

FURMENTY

(we never called it Frumenty)

Made by soaking wheat in water overnight and then simmering it in milk until tender. Before serving, cinnamon, sugar and brandy are added to taste. Allow 2oz of grain per person and about a pint of milk to 8oz of wheat initially, adding more milk if necessary over a period of an hour or two of cooking.

YULE CAKES

Take 1lb of plain flour. Rub in ¼lb of butter, margarine or lard and add 5oz of sugar. Stir round and make a hollow in the centre. Work together 1oz of yeast with 1 teaspoon of sugar until it goes runny and then add ⅔ of a teacup of lukewarm water. Pour this mixture into the hollow, stir in a little of the flour and scatter more over the batter. Set to rise in a warm place for about 20 minutes. Prepare ¾lb currants and sultanas, and ¼lb mixed peel. Warm ¼ pint of milk and add a beaten egg to it. Measure 1 teaspoon mixed spice and 1 teaspoon cinnamon. Work all these ingredients into a

dough and leave it to rise for an hour. Divide into about 18 cakes and put them to rise for about 20 minutes on greased trays. Bake at Regulo 5, 375°, for about 30 minutes.

The dough being a slack one, it is not always possible to knead it in the conventional manner. It may require to be stirred with a spoon and a little more flour added so that it can be handled for making the cakes. There is a tendency in baking for the fruit to burn, so do not have the oven too hot and reduce the temperature a little if necessary.

*   *   *   *

THE frumenty is served first, hot. The cooled Yule Cakes are set on a dish near a small round whole cheese with a sprig of holly stuck in the top. Before the cheese is cut into, the holly sprig is laid aside—to be kept for use on the pudding on Christmas Day. The top surface of the cheese is marked with a cross using the rounded tip of a knife sideways to make a broad mark. The Yule Cakes are buttered and eaten with cheese.

It would seem that this custom can be traced back for at least 200 years and is an unbroken one over the past 100 years in my own family.

*   *   *   *

After the simplicity of the Christmas Eve supper—the fast before the feast—tradition continued with the Christmas Day food. The turkey had a thyme and lemon stuffing only and was served with mashed potatoes, brussel sprouts, and the usual bacon rolls, little sausages and breadsauce. The pudding had been made long before and stirred by members of the household, each with a secret wish. It must have been a major operation in the days when ready washed and seeded fruit and chopped peel and suet could not be bought. Several puddings were made, one of which was used at New Year.

CHRISTMAS PUDDING

(enough for 4 large puddings)
Mix together 1lb chopped or grated suet with ½lb plain flour and 1lb sieved breadcrumbs. Prepare 1½ seeded (Lexia) raisins by chopping small and add 1lb sultanas, 1lb currants and ½lb mixed peel. Combine with the dry ingredients along with 1lb soft brown sugar and make a hollow in the middle. Beat up 8 eggs and pour them into the hollow along with the grated rind of one lemon and one orange, the juice of half a lemon and half an orange, 1 grated nutmeg and ½ pint of brandy.

Stir very well and pack into greased basins, tie down and boil for 8 hours. Leave some weeks before use. Steam for a further 4 hours before serving turned out on a dish with a sprig of holly in the top. No sauce of any sort was provided but some of the family liked to add a little granulated sugar to their helpings to give a gritty contrast.

*   *   *

AFTER the turkey and pudding there was dessert. In my mother's youth she remembered that this included not only mince pies but also the Christmas Cake along with the nuts, tangerines, crystallised fruit, dates, figs and chocolates. Ginger wine was used to drink 'The Health of All Present and Absent', before the crackers were pulled and people helped themselves to their choice of the good things.

MINCE PIES

The mince pies were always made in little oval patty tins—Manger shaped—and were of short

pastry. The 'receipt' for the mincemeat makes 4lb and keeps well.

A lemon put to simmer till tender (as for making marmalade). Meanwhile a basin is filled with 1lb chopped seeded (Lexia) raisins, 1lb currants, 1lb white sugar, and 1lb cooking apples (weighed before peeling and chopping; use ones that 'fall' easily), ¼lb mixed peel and the juice and rind of a fresh lemon. The cooked lemon is cut up, the seeds discarded and the pulp and peel added to the rest of the ingredients along with up to a teacupful of brandy. After stirring well the mincemeat is put in jars and stored till needed.

*   *   *

FINALLY, well before Christmas, the cake was made.

CHRISTMAS CAKE

The original recipe for the 'Pound Cake' says 'take 8 eggs, and their weight in butter, sugar and flour', but as eggs vary in size it is necessary to weigh them and use as many as it takes to make 16oz before cracking them and beating them up in a bowl. Cream 1lb butter (margarine in these days), add 1lb white sugar and beat well. Gradually beat in the eggs and stir in 2 tablespoons of brandy (or 2 drops each of almond, lemon and vanilla essences). Sift 1lb plain flour and add a little at a time and then stir in 1lb sultanas mixed with ¾lb currants and ¼lb mixed peel plus ¼ to ½lb washed dried glace cherries. Bake in a lined tin for up to 4 hours at Regulo 1 - 2 (275° - 300°F). A sixpence used to be included in the cake.

Icing: About December 23rd the stored cake was iced.

Crush 1lb of almonds with pestle and mortar, and add 8oz of icing sugar. This is moistened with enough triple strength orangeflower water to make it bind together (2 tablespoonsful can safely be added to begin with and more put in, or use plain water till it is possible to work the almond paste over the cake with the hands. It is not rolled out or stuck on with jam.) Of course ground almonds can be used now these are available. This amount is enough for the top and sides of the cake. The almond paste is covered with a thin layer of white icing made by sieving 6oz icing sugar and stirring in a little hot water to the right consistency to spread over the cake. The next day 10oz icing sugar is mixed to a thickish cream with triple strength rose water and spread on for the final layer before decorating. Silver balls, angelica and cherries can be used and perhaps a china snowman.

* * * * * *

AS with the Christmas Eve supper, the dinner was also eaten by candlelight making the whole festival a magic and special time, full of the family traditional cooking and customs to link together the universal and worldwide celebrations of the birth of the Baby of Bethlehem, so far away from Yorkshire.

Two Christmas Recipes
by Dalesman readers
(see photos on pages 47 and 48)

CHRISTMAS BISCUITS

Fig. 7

4oz self-raising flour
1oz castor sugar
1 egg
2oz butter or margarine
Pinch of salt
Drinking chocolate
Icing sugar
Coconut
Silver balls
Cherries
Chocolate buttons
100s and 1,000s

Measure out the self-raising flour and sugar. Put them into a big basin together with a pinch of salt and the butter or margarine. Now rub together the flour, fat and sugar. Do it with your fingertips until there are no more lumps of fat left in the flour.

Next put in the flavour you want. Two spoons of coconut if you want coconut biscuits, or 1 spoon of drinking chocolate powder and one drop of vanilla essence if you want chocolate biscuits.

Now take the small basin and the egg. Break the egg into the small basin and beat it up with the whisk. Take 2 dessertspoons of the egg, add to the flour and stir until it forms one lump, firm but not sticky. If it is too dry, put in some more egg. Take your rolling pin, sprinkle flour onto the rolling pin and on the table or pastry board. Put the lump of dough on the board and roll out until it is thin. Take your cutters and cut out all the shapes, putting them on to a greased tray as you cut them. Gather up the bits, pat them together, roll out and make more biscuits. Put the baking tin into the middle of the oven (355°F or gas Mark 4) and cook for about 12 minutes. Take them out and cool on a wire tray.

Decorate with icing sugar mixed with butter, which is called butter cream. You make it like this: Measure 4oz butter and sift 6oz icing sugar. Cream the butter and gradually add the sifted icing sugar to it. Beat until it is white and very creamy. Divide into three or four different portions and make each a different colour. Wet a knife in hot water and spread these on the biscuits and decorate with silver balls, cherries or chocolate buttons to make them even prettier. (Don't eat too much of the butter cream or you won't have enough to put on the biscuits!)

CHRISTMAS PASTRIES
Fig. 8

1 x 7oz packet frozen puff pastry, thawed
1 egg
5oz ground almonds
3oz caster sugar
2oz icing sugar
1 tablespoon lemon juice
1-2 drops almond essence
1 egg, beaten for glazing

Roll out pastry to an oblong about 15in x 8in. Trim edges and cut into 8in x 2½in strips. Beat egg until just frothy. Add ground almonds, sugars, lemon juice and almond essence and mix to a smooth paste. Roll into long sausage shapes about ¾in thick. Cut almond filling into same lengths as pastry strips. Wrap pastry round filling seal edges and ends with beaten egg. Shape into letters to represent the initial of the family name. Place on a baking sheet and brush with beaten egg. Bake in a hot oven, 425°F or gas Mark 7, for 25 minutes until golden brown. Cool. Makes 6 letters.

Index

Meat Dishes

Beef Mould	65
Beef Roll	12
Beef Steak Pudding	64
Brisket of Beef	11
Dumpling Toppers	39
Meat Balls	37
Roast Duckling	37
Steak Casserole	67
Upside-Down Pie	49
Yorkshire Goose Pie	66
Yorkshireman's Goose	49

Pickles

Pickled Mushrooms	31
Pickled Walnuts	32
Samphire Pickle	57

Preserves

Blackcurrant Jam	30
Bramble Mould	30
Crab Apple and Bramble Jelly	28
Lemon Curd	27

Marrow, Lemon and Ginger Jam	28
Orange Curd	27
Rowan Jelly	57

Puddings and Sweets

Apple Pie	51
Cheese and Curd Tart	51
Christmas Pudding	73
Cranberry and Apple Mousse	40
Lemon Delight	19
Meringues	25
Othellos and Desdemonas	26
Pineapple Pudding	17
Plum Pudding	17
Summer Pudding	16

Salad Dressings

Mushroom Ketchup	31
Salad Dressing	27

Savouries and starters

Bean Pie	62
Black Pudding	61
Cheese Souffle	61
Cheese Straws	15
Cornish Pasties	62
Creole Eggs	50
Dock Pudding	55
Frumenty	72
Meat Jelly Pie	13
Onion Toast	67
Potato Jane	64
Potato Pancakes	62
Potted Meat	15
Roll-Burger Picnic	40
Sausage Mould	68
Sausage Rolls	64
Sausage Savoury	68
Savoury Meat Roll	67
Savoury Pudding	65
Stuffed Tomatoes	65
Yorkshire Pudding	50

Spices and Herbs 33